Film Noir

and

Technicolor Characters

Timothy Cobb Fine Arts
January 13–February 3, 2017

©2016 Timothy Cobb Fine Arts

Book design by Colleen Kassner

"Film Noir and Technicolor Characters"
Timothy Cobb Fine Arts

John Balsley, "Heroic Assemblages"
Mixed media sculpture

Jeff Darrow, "Film Noir Stars"
Acrylic and charcoal on canvas paintings

Colleen Kassner, "Technicolor Characters"
Oil paintings

Philo Kassner, "Bohemians"
Black and White Silver Gelatin Photographs

Michael Kutzer, "Punch"
Woodcut Prints

Michael Thompson, "Taxi Cabs, Amusement Rides, and Hypnosis"
Mixed media Sculpture

● ● ● ● ● ● ● ● ● ● ● ● ● ● ● ● ● ● ●

It's all the Kassners' fault.

About a year ago an artsy couple came into the gallery. It was just the three of us. I recognize artists by the way they look at art; each knew art. We admired good paintings together for some time before I asked if they were artists. Colleen called herself a painter, and Philo a photographer. I asked them if they were represented by a gallery in Milwaukee—they were not. Mind you, they didn't present themselves as pushy artists looking for representation; no cell phones were yanked out of a pocket to bluster through pictures of their art. I asked them why they hadn't. "It's disrespectful!" Colleen quipped. That's old school. Game on.

A few days later I found myself in their living room—the opening scene to a story that unfolded over the next year.

The Kassners, each in their own way, had dedicated themselves to documenting the art world's "underground" in Milwaukee, WI. Colleen in her oil paintings of local artists I call "Technicolor Characters," Philo in his atmospheric black and white photographs—8,000 of them captured over several decades. Here was a good start to an exhibition. As a curator I knew I was on my way, but had no idea how lightning bolts were to strike four more times, high winds coaxing wonderful artists my way.

The next scene introduced my friend Jeff Darrow stopping in for a visit and carrying paintings he'd recently finished. Jeff is a gifted artist with a most painterly touch. He pulled out a painting of Clark Gable, *en grisaille*, and told me he was working on a series of paintings of actors from the Film Noir era. Lightning bolt! "The uh, stuff that dreams are made of." (Spade, Maltese Falcon, 1941.)

I recently renovated the front of the gallery as a showcase for sculpture, and plan for partnering two and three dimensional work for each exhibition. I had no gallery artists who were producing work that would make sense for our burgeoning exhibition, nor did I know of anyone in the realm of possibility. Enter Google and Michael Thompson.

My first thought was sculpture made of movie film, and then came reels, projector parts, or scripts-something related to production. Perhaps set models, furnishings, back drops or architecture; costumes? I always loved the look of art deco buildings in black and white films. I researched each one of those areas, and in doing so up popped a photo of a sculpture of a deco-looking building made of vintage erector set pieces with a beacon on top sporting a glass dome. And, it was a working lamp! Mood lighting—movie mood lighting—Lightning bolt!

I went to Thompson's website and found a treasure trove of 3-D work by an artist-maker of true, creative vision. There it was—another erector set lamp with a lighted sign that once sat atop a cab: "TAXI". As Colleen quickly pointed out, what Film Noir great doesn't have a leggy lady exiting a cab on a rainy night, light aglow? I visited his studio and chose eleven pieces for the exhibition.

The erector set buildings reminded me of the old King Kong flicks, the deco design at the peak of the Empire State building, Kong swatting at the plane, villains, super heroes flying in to save the day.

Lightning bolt! John Balsley…another great, "I HAVE to make things," guy with a serious imagination. One of his flying men-of course! Masterpieces constructed from found objects. My favorite is hanging in his den. Will he let me have it? Yes. What does he call it? He didn't have a title. I'm calling it "The Avenger"…

The cherry on top came with a series of woodcuts by the Milwaukee based German-American artist Michael Kutzer. They feature the character Punch, the rascal partner to Judy, whom together form the popular duo Punch and Judy. The work ties together the Noir and Technicolor themes in the artist's ingenious use of black, white and red inks. The work betrays Kutzer's deep, traditional, European training.

(Fade to black…orchestra plays)

THE END

John Balsley

"Heroic Assemblage"

My career has encompassed an amalgam of materials and processes ensuing painting, sculpture, collage, assemblage, drawing, and installation work.

Concerning my choice of subject matter I am fascinated by the incredibleness of natural phenomena. I enjoy my freedom to abstract and invent my own rules. I believe the impact of a work of art is not only the immediate experience, that of being detained, but also the impact of memory to revisit the phenomenon of that initial experience.

For the most part, I've always been attracted to art that is brave and on the edge. I've been engrossed by art that took chances by joining impossibilities and by exploring and embracing the unexpected: art that is made manifest, ostensibly, by a great amount of effort, conviction, and experience from and of its maker.

Art is always a testimony, reflecting its maker's integrity and marriage to and in concert with its dedication and powerful ideas.

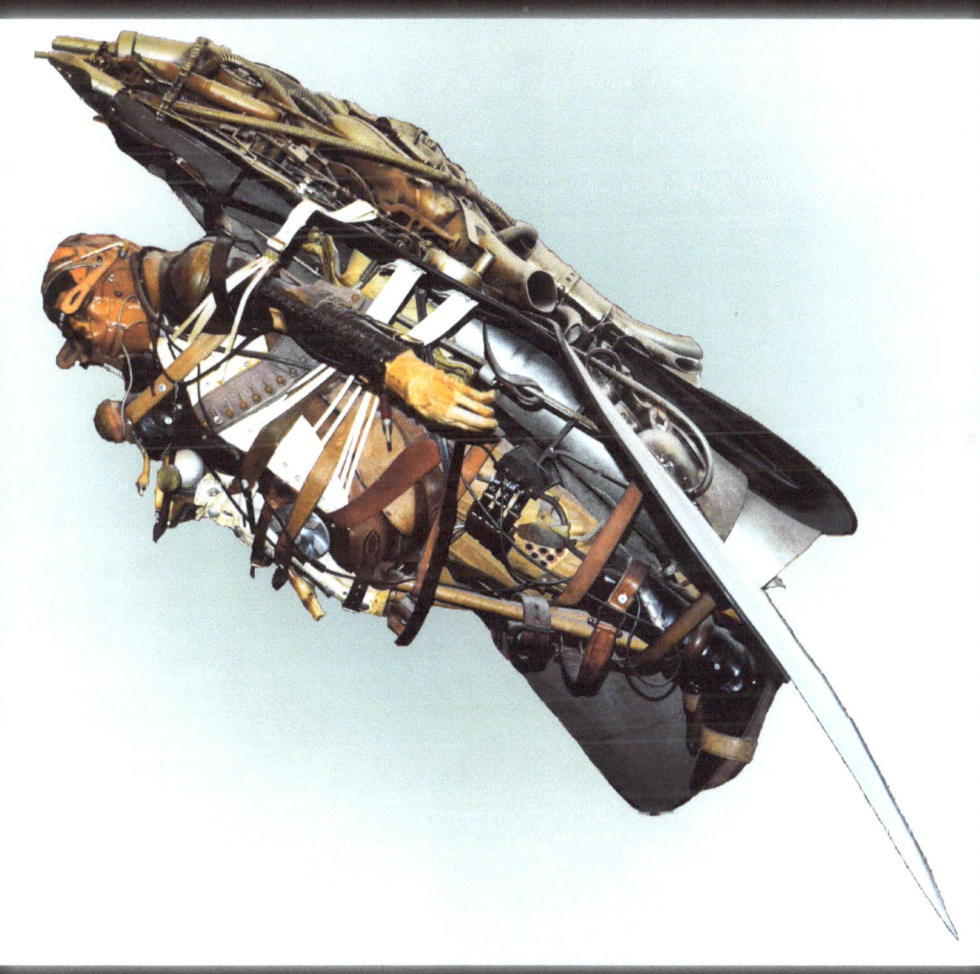

The Avenger

36" W X 58" H X 22" D

Mixed Media

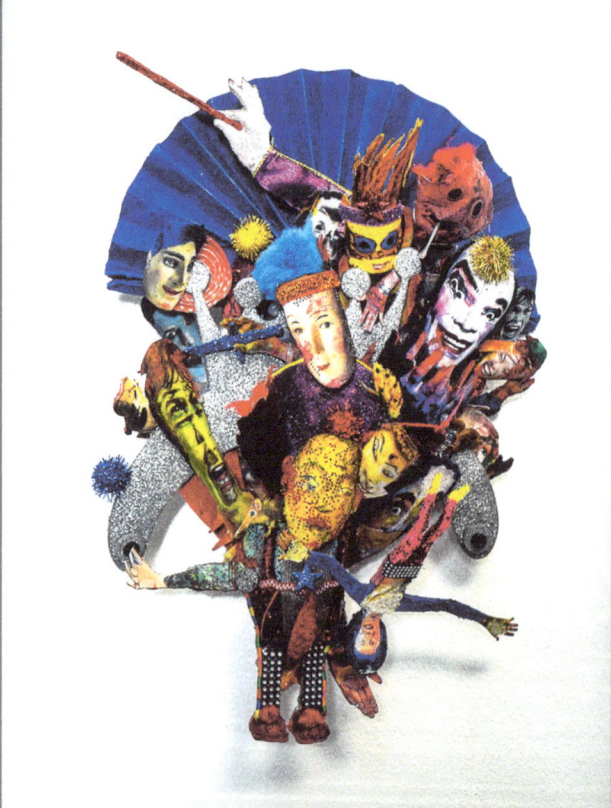

THE DIRECTOR'S DREAM

11" W X 16" H X 9" D

MIXED MEDIA

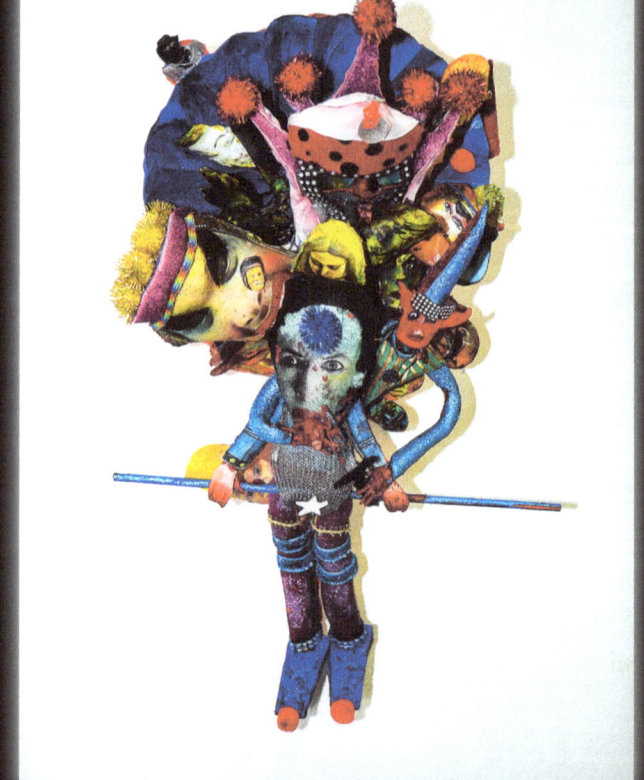

THE ILLUSIONIST'S DREAM

10" W X 17" H X 9" D

MIXED MEDIA

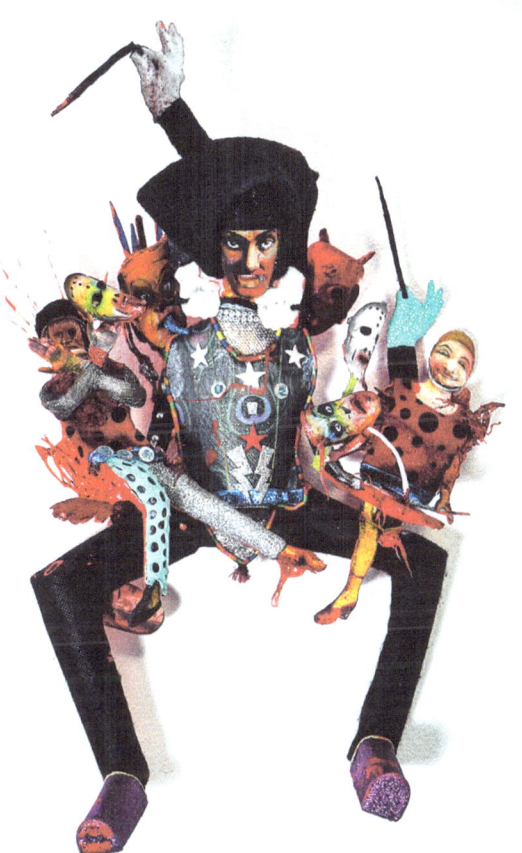

THE MAGICIAN'S DREAM
13" W x 20" H x 6" D

MIXED MEDIA

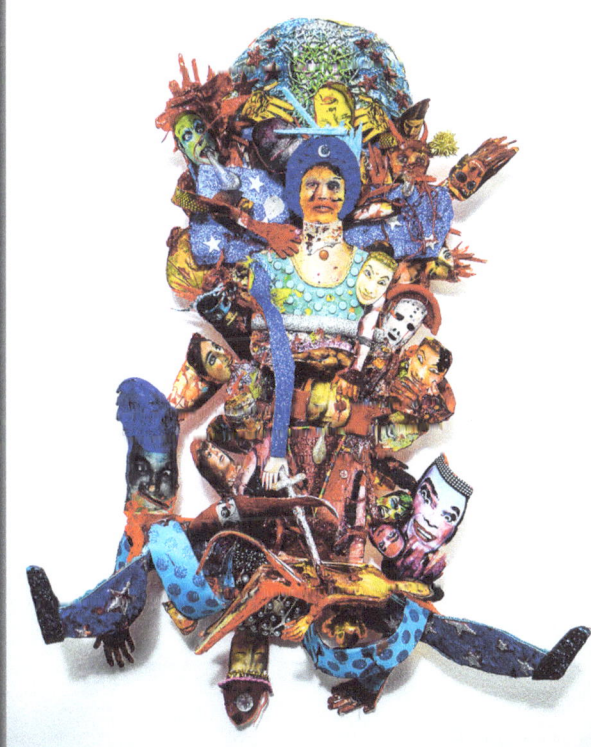

THE DANCER'S DREAM
18" W x 23" H x 7.5" D

MIXED MEDIA

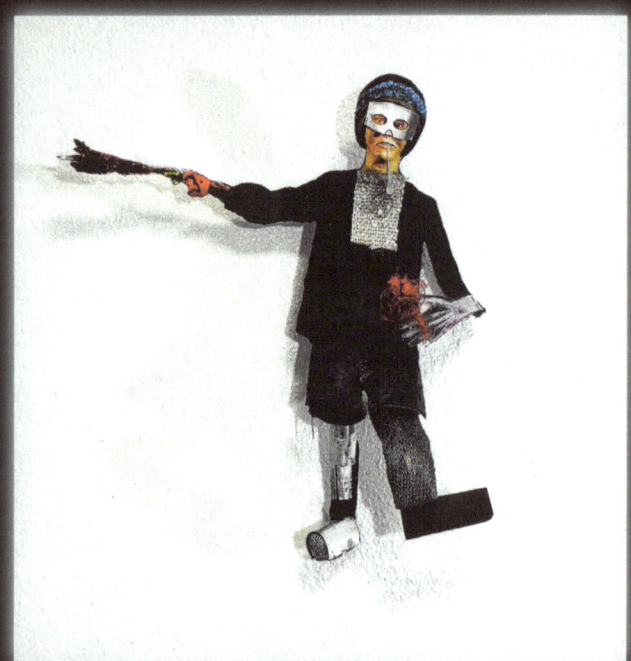

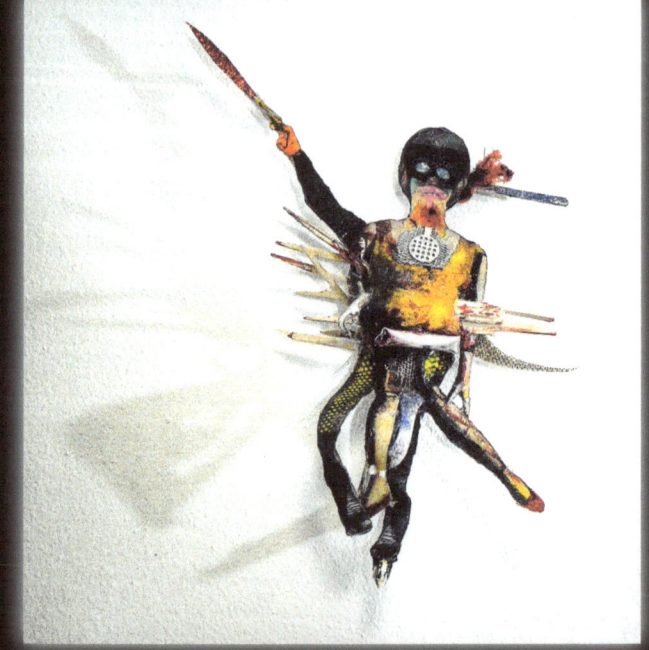

VICTORY

8" H x 9" W x 3" D

MIXED MEDIA

THE EVENING NEWS

8" W x 10" H x 3.5" D

MIXED MEDIA

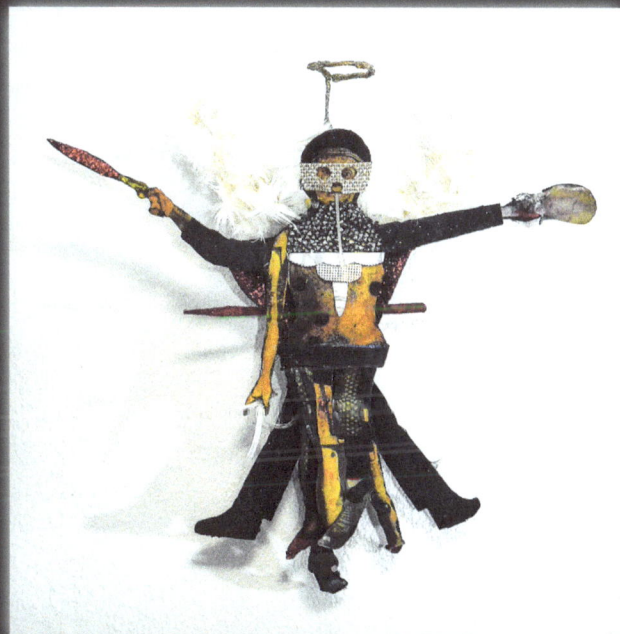

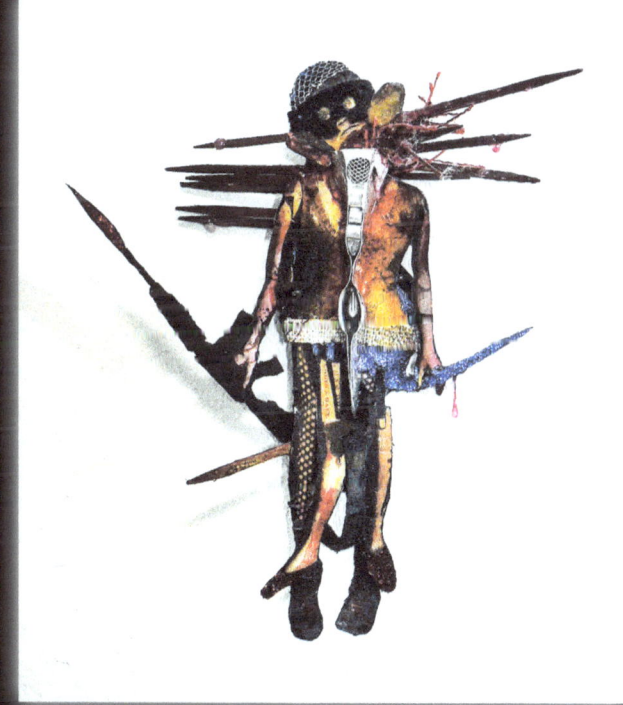

CINEMA
11" W x 10.5" H x 3" D
MIXED MEDIA

Allegiance
9" H x 9.5" W x 3.5" D
MIXED MEDIA

Jeff Darrow was raised, along with his nine siblings on a dairy farm near Shullsburg, a community in southwest Wisconsin. His father saw to it that hard work was a preamble to breakfast and other meals, so Darrow developed a farmer's work ethic and a love for, among other things, dirt-floor machine sheds full of heavy rusted things and sunbaked landscapes. He began to draw partly to escape the boredom of daily farm chores and watching the corn grow. During those long, hot summer days in rural America, it was his sense that everything seemed to stand still and change came grudgingly slow that inspired him. Although he tries to capture that same stillness in his work, he tackles the subject matter now with urgency, before it is reduced to scrap iron, parking lots or condos.

"Many insights have been published about the Film Noir style, so I'll break no new ground here. It has had an influence on countless artists for decades and has been inspired by film's greatest talents. Its darkness, both in value and mood, has helped shape our visual arts for many years. My portraits are a celebration of some of the actors who are, literally, the faces of Film Noir. In this HDMI, computer generated world of digital media and entertainment, these hard-boiled countenances are slowly being forgotten. This is my way of pushing back."

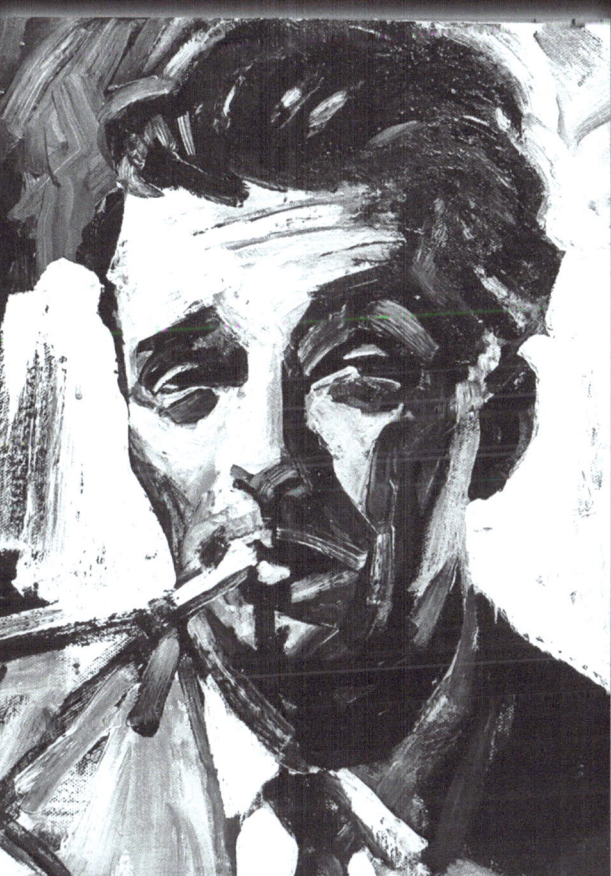

ROBERT

16" H x 12" W

ACRYLIC AND CHARCOAL ON CANVAS

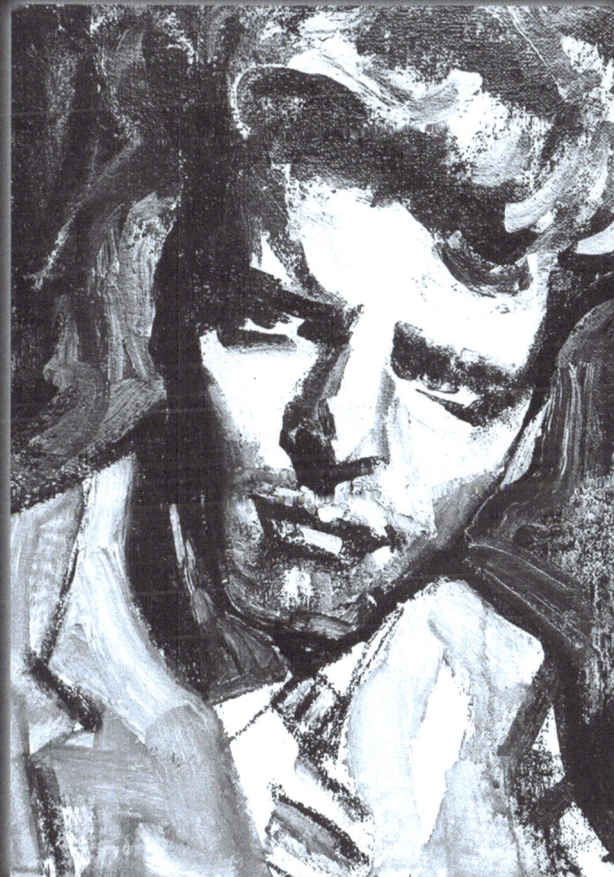

BURT

16" H x 12" W

ACRYLIC AND CHARCOAL ON CANVAS

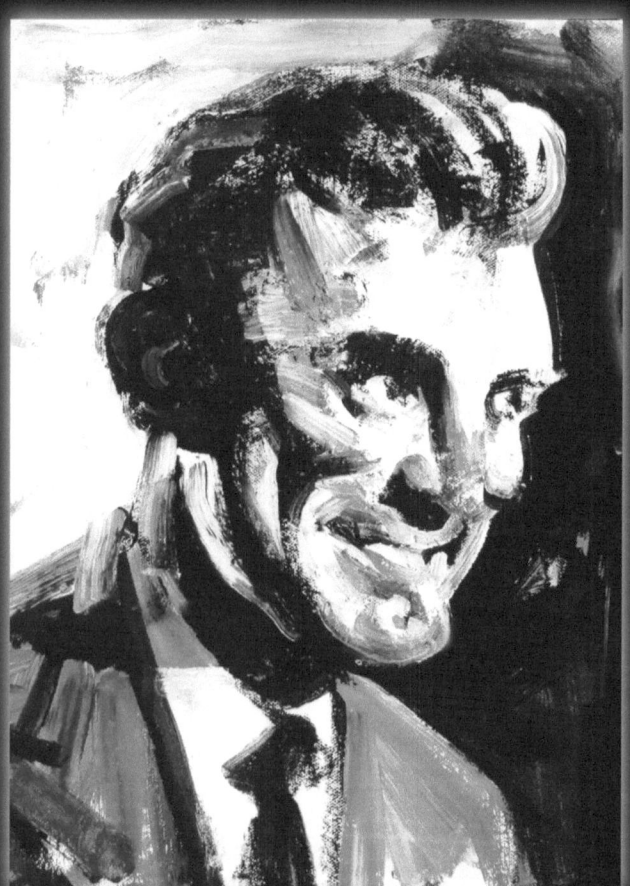

Kirk

16" H X 12" W

ACRYLIC AND CHARCOAL ON CANVAS

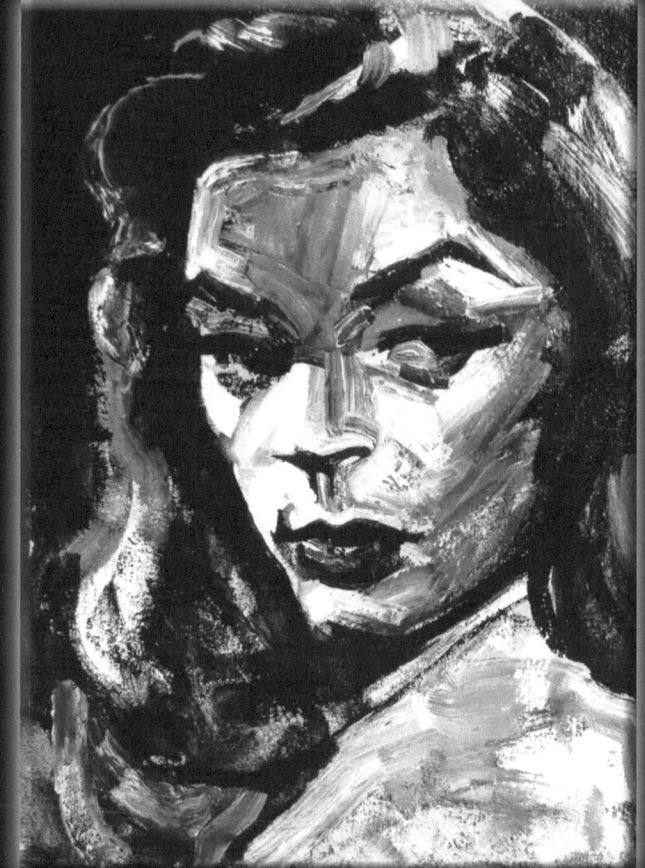

LAUREN

16" H X 12" W

ACRYLIC AND CHARCOAL ON CANVAS

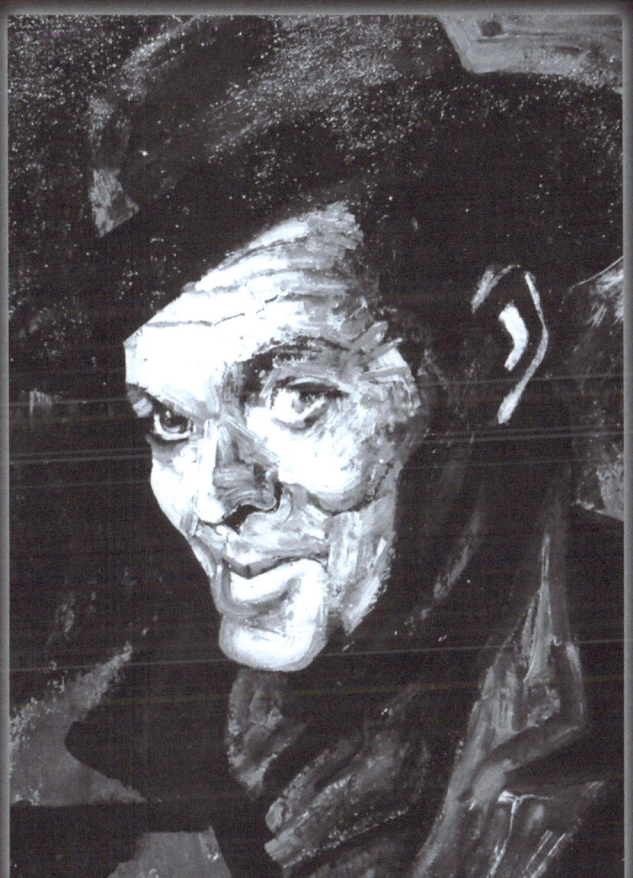

RAY

16" H x 12" W

ACRYLIC AND CHARCOAL ON CANVAS

ORSON

16" H x 12" W

ACRYLIC AND CHARCOAL ON CANVAS

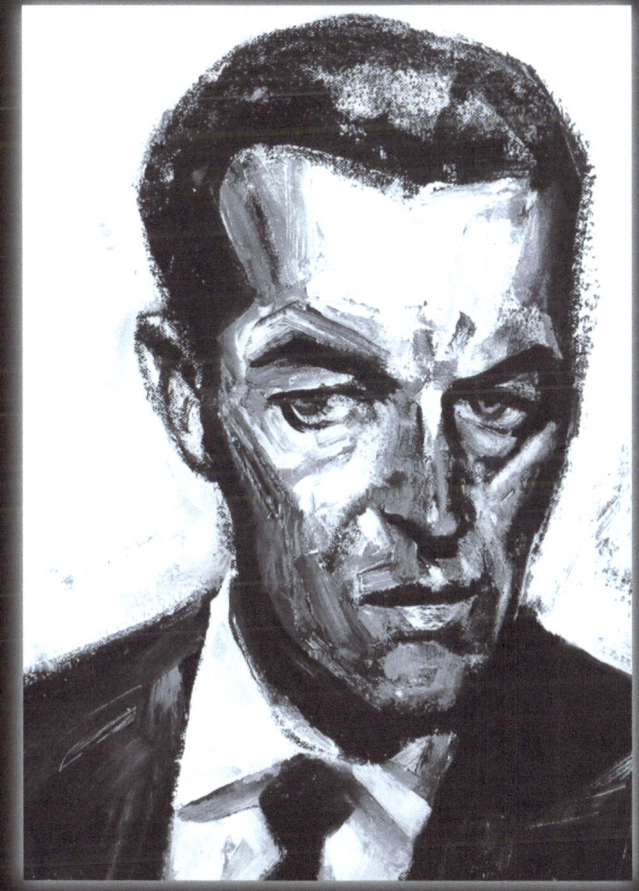

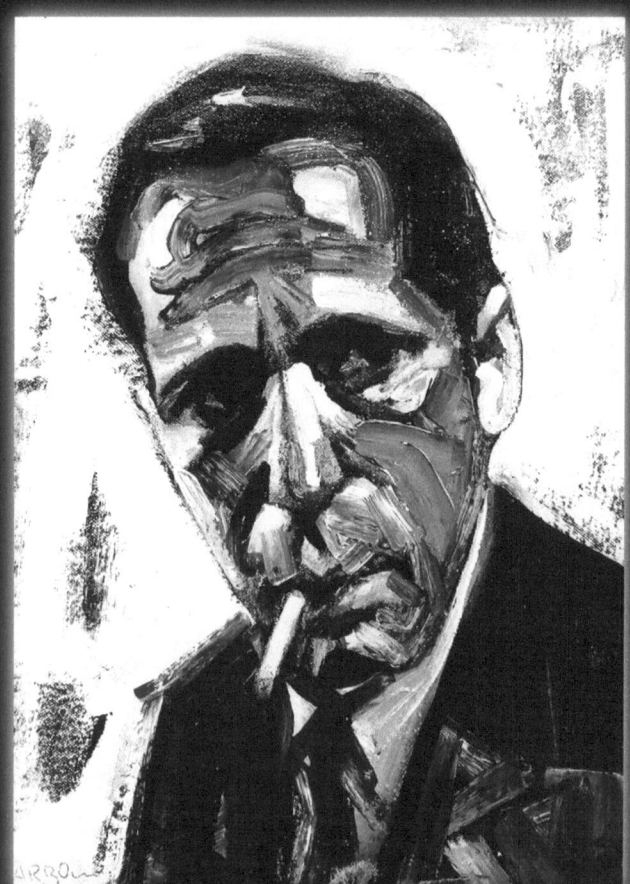

Humphrey

16" H x 12" W

Acrylic and charcoal on canvas

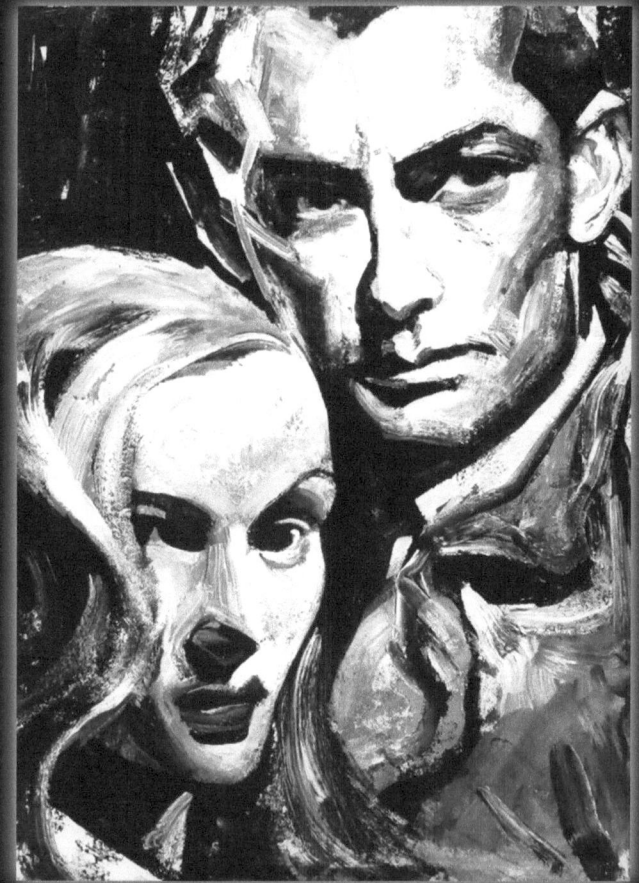

Veronica and Alan

16" H x 12" W

Acrylic and charcoal on canvas

My creative years began as a writer. Lesson number one was, "Write what you know." That lesson is carried forward into my painting. I paint who and what is familiar; the beauty in lives of fellow artists, bohemians, and eccentrics. Whether painters, photographers, musicians, or appreciators of such, capturing what is underneath the social exterior is my goal. Sometimes the person is portrayed in a humorous vein, sometimes seriously, and sometimes as a person of deep beauty, whether male or female. Portraiture is one of my modes of creation. It records for history the image of a person in a manner that is time honored.

The other lesson as a writer was, "Create mood and environment." My newest work, *The Ghosts of Goldmann's*, transfers my literary lessons to the visual realm. Assembled in the painting are a rag-tag collection of friends and associates at the remnants of the lunch counter from Goldmann's Department Store on Mitchel Street. The store dates back into the 1930's and remained a family business until its closure in 2007.

In December of 2015, it was casually mentioned by a friend that the original lunch counter was housed in a Milwaukee warehouse. My jaw dropped, my eyes widened and I immediately knew that it had to be painted. An inquiry was made to the owner of the warehouse to see if I could do a photo shoot at the lunch counter. Happily, he approved. A crew of friends, my daughter, her boyfriend, and my husband descended upon the warehouse to produce the reference photos. Although much of the original layout of the lunch counter was gone, the essence remained and is captured in this painting. Replicating the original diner on canvas wasn't the goal. I sought to create the image of a memory…of a time long passed and dearly loved.

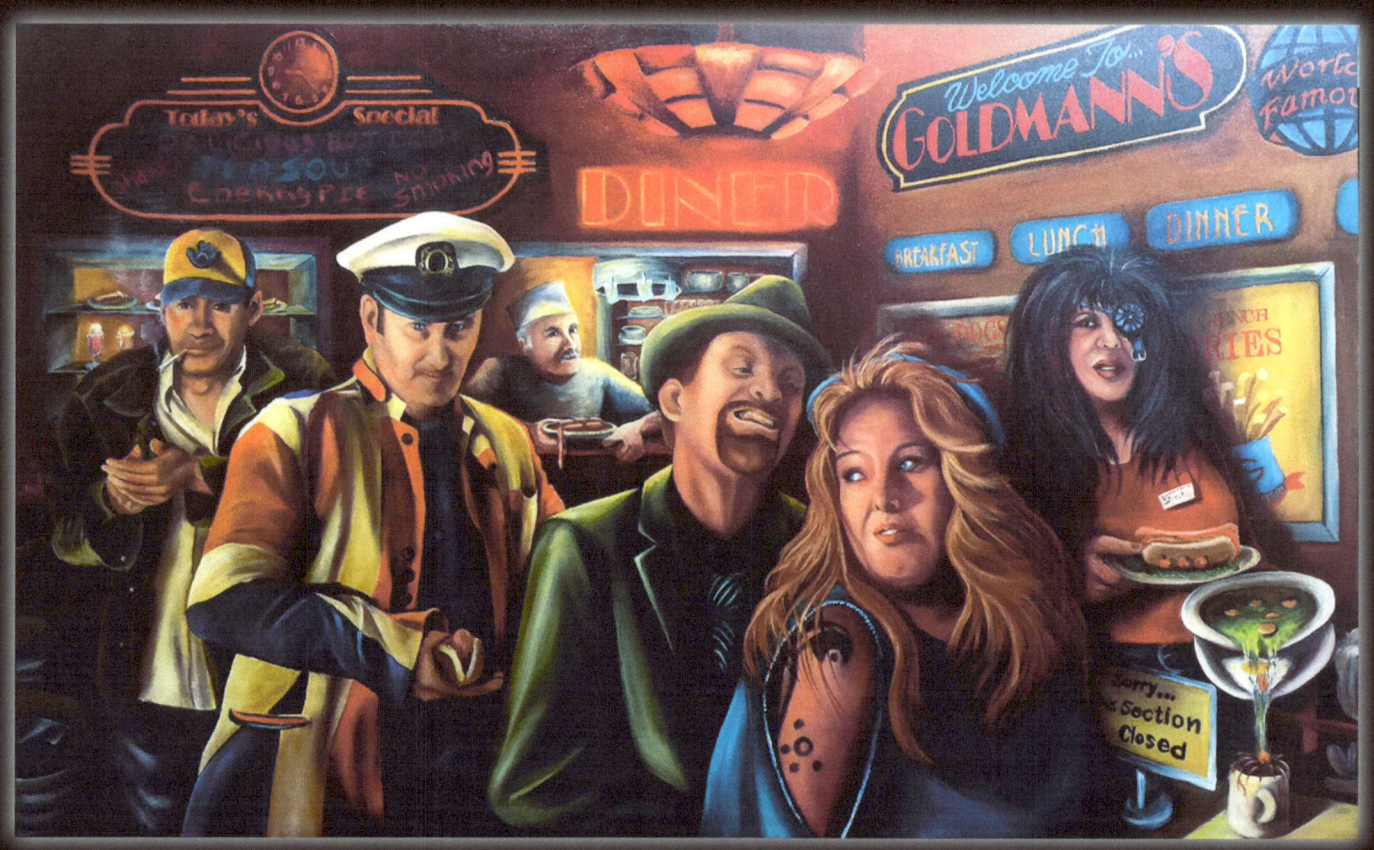

The Ghosts of Goldmann's

36" H x 60" W

OIL ON INFRASTRUCTURE CANVAS

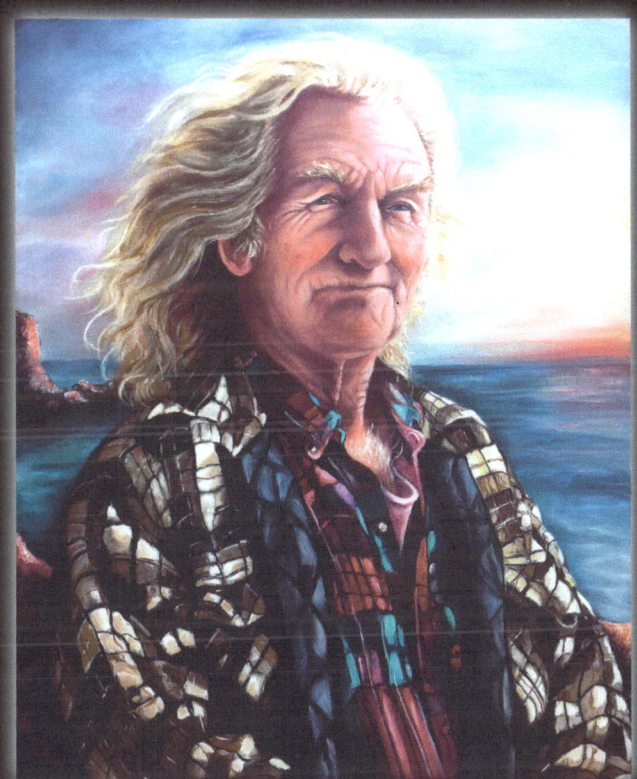

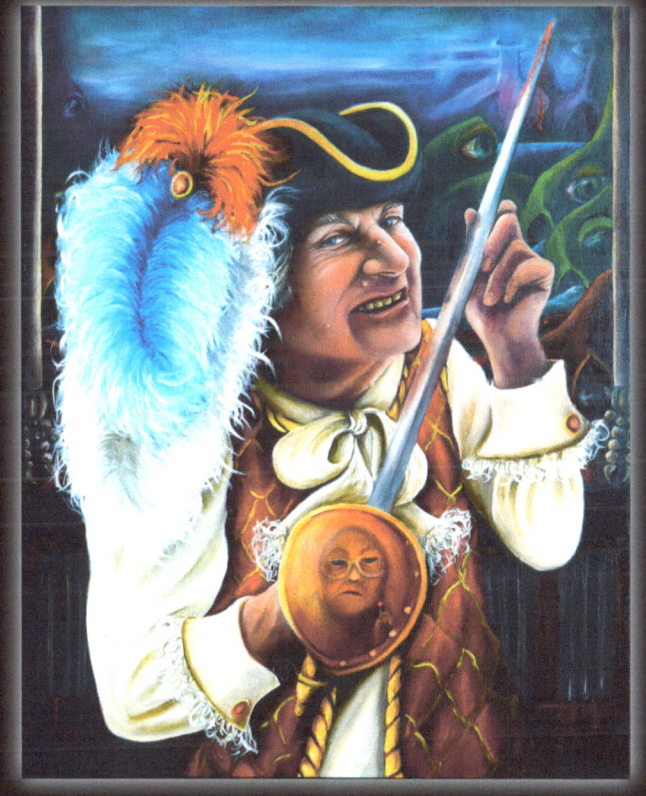

Michael "Ringo" White
Viking Soul
30" H x 24" W
OIL ON BIRCH PANEL

Francis Ford
Don Giovanni Wannabe
30" H x 24" W
OIL ON BIRCH PANEL

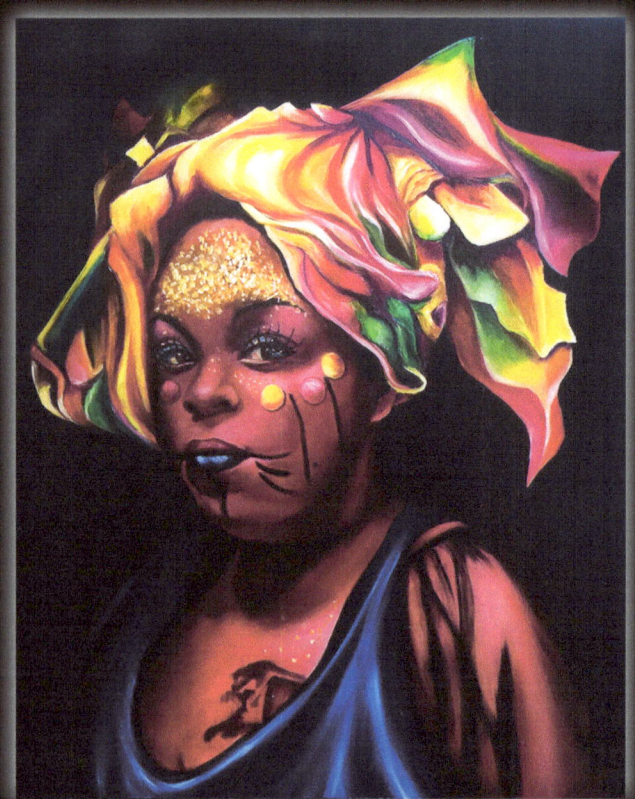

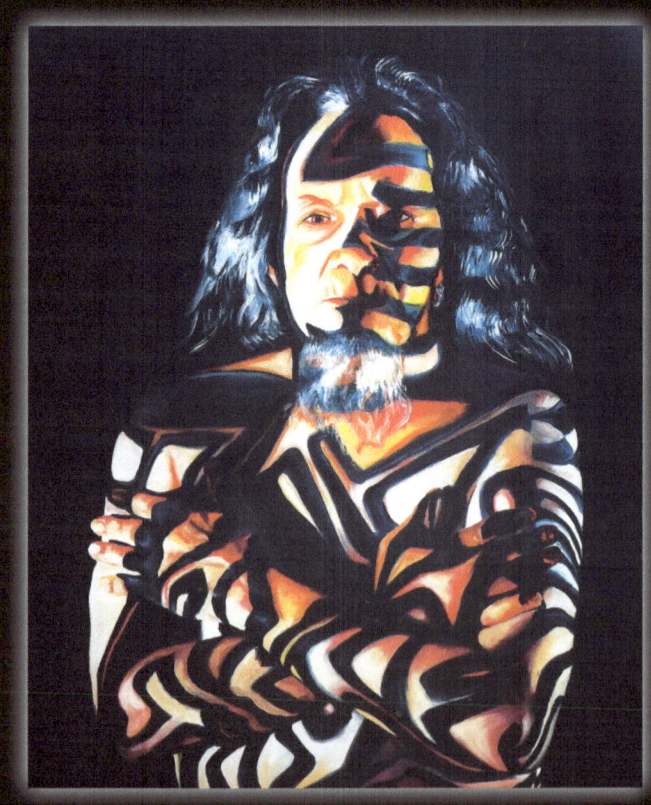

Ingrid Eubanks
China Allure
30" H x 24" W
OIL ON BIRCH PANEL

Michael R. Flasch
The Table is Turned
30" H x 24" W
OIL ON BIRCH PANEL

Rosemary Ollison
Baubles and Bangles
30" H x 24" W

OIL ON BIRCH PANEL

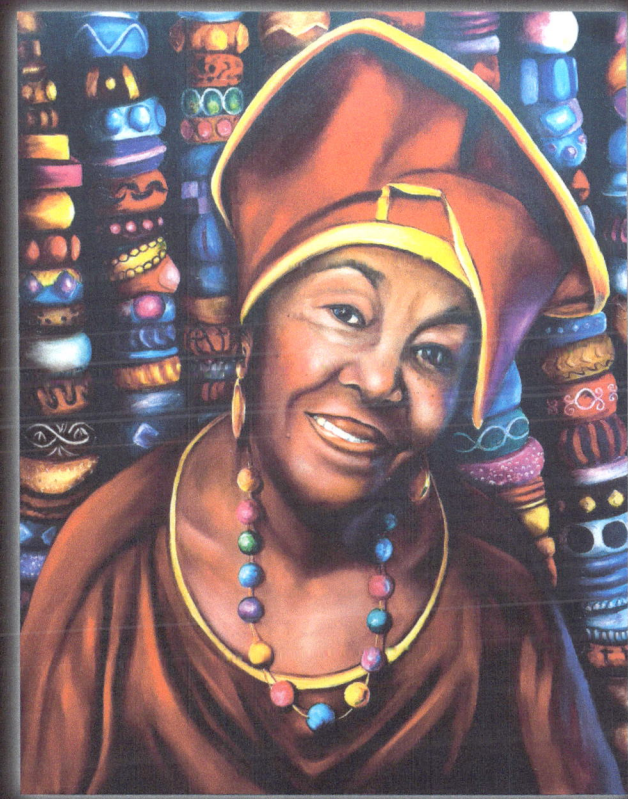

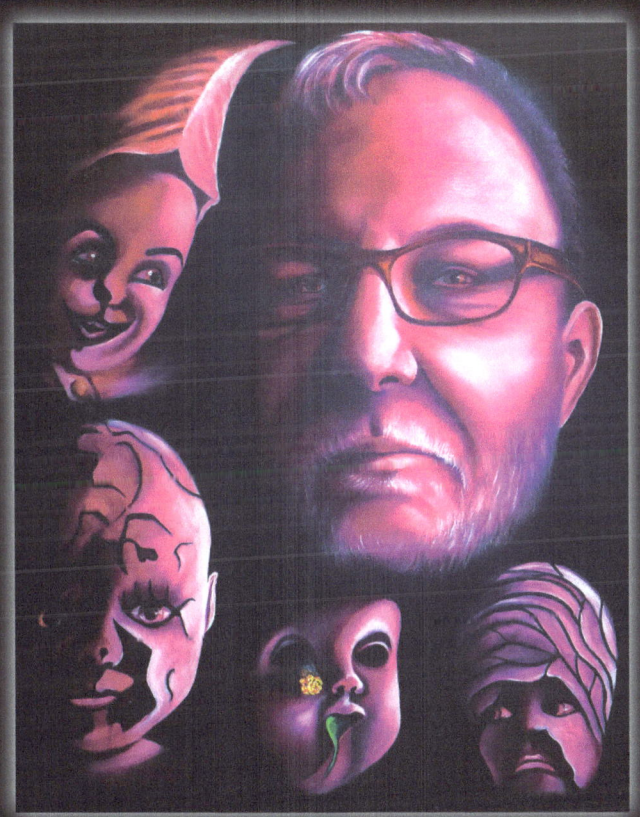

Bill Zuback
Hello, Dollies
30" H x 24" W

OIL ON BIRCH PANEL

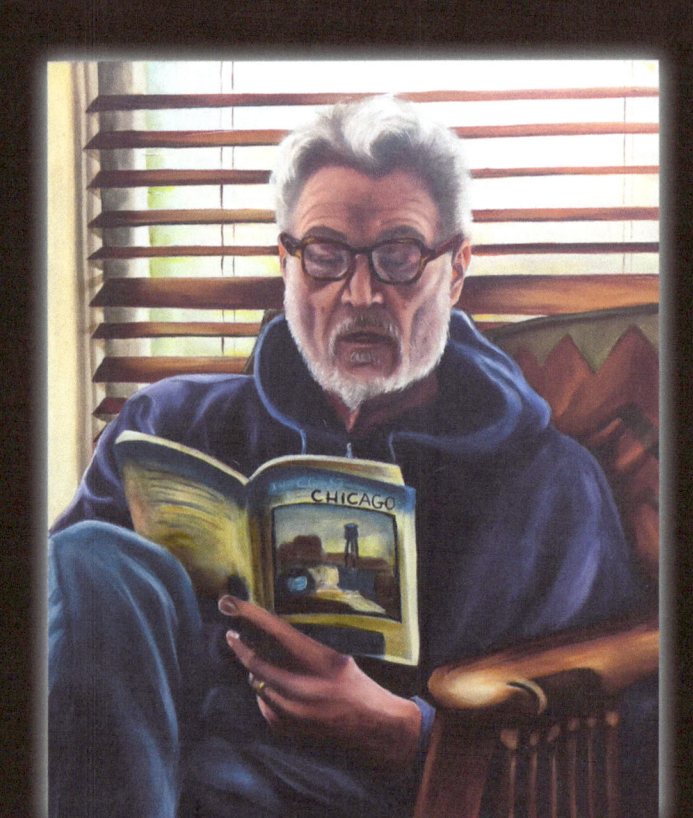

"Bohemians"

• • • • • • • • • • • • • • • • •

At age six my parents gave me a "Roy Rogers" camera. Loading and winding the film was simple enough, but I could not understand why the camera did not see things the way I did.

For my seventh birthday I was given a "real" camera, a Kodak Brownie. The pictures turned out! The camera stayed with me through high school, my first few years of college, and was with me when inducted into the Army. Photography seemed little more than a hobby.

My neophyte status ended in 1970, at the age of twenty-one, while I was stationed in Germany. I spent $147 of my $249 a month pay to purchase a 35mm Pentax at the PX. Quite a few of my fellow soldiers did the same. As long as our air defense unit made its presence known to the nearby Soviet forces, it was not considered goofing off to go out and use our cameras during normal working hours. Better still, there was a well-equipped darkroom on-base that we were free to use.

I carry what I learned in the army with me throughout my photography. During the ensuing years my technique has improved, I've adjusted to newer technology, and I never lost my love of capturing a person in a candid moment.

For "Film Noir and Technicolor Characters" I combine photos from earlier film work with digital photos of contemporary people in classic settings. All the images seen in the exhibit are printed traditionally with silver gelatin.

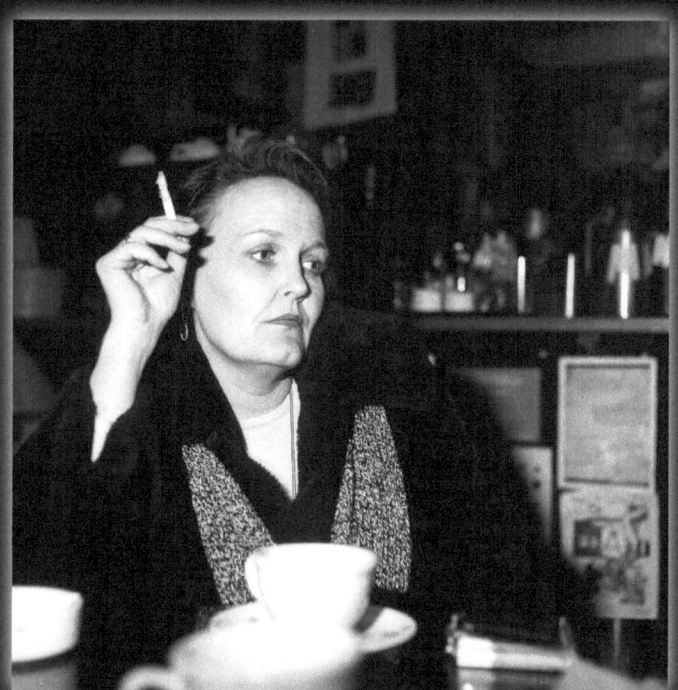

Coffee Ennui

IMAGE SIZE: 16" H X 16" W

SILVER GELATIN PRINT

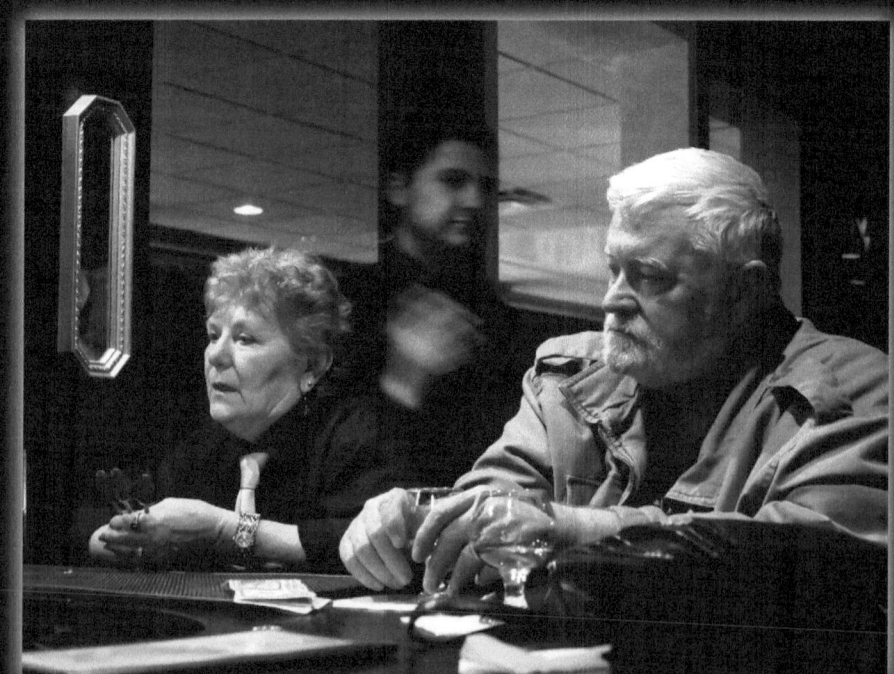

Hob Nob

IMAGE SIZE 14.5" H X 19.375" W

SILVER GELATIN PRINT

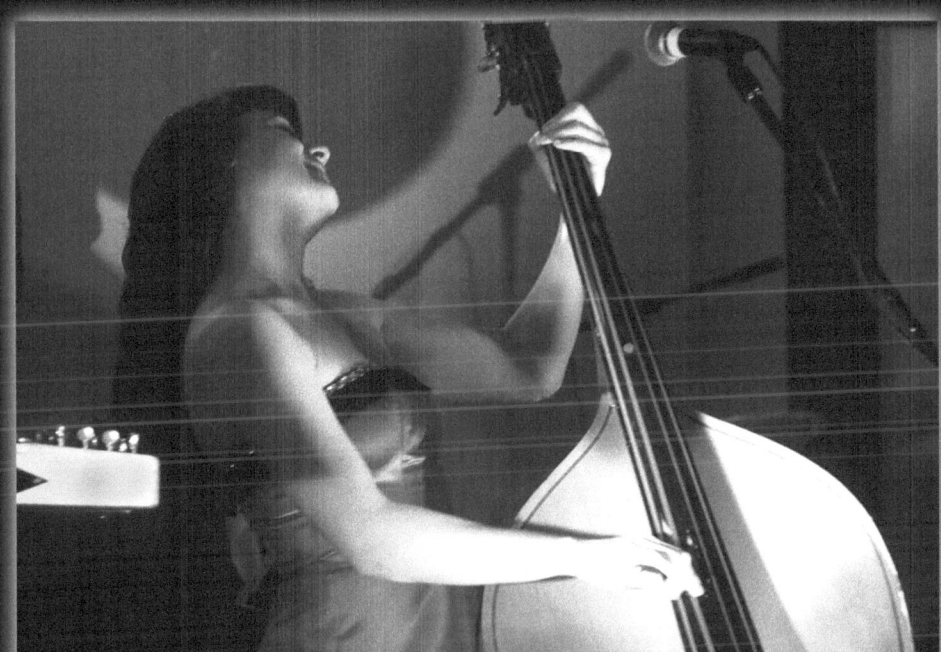

Delilah DeWylde

IMAGE SIZE 13" H X 19.375" W

SILVER GELATIN PRINT

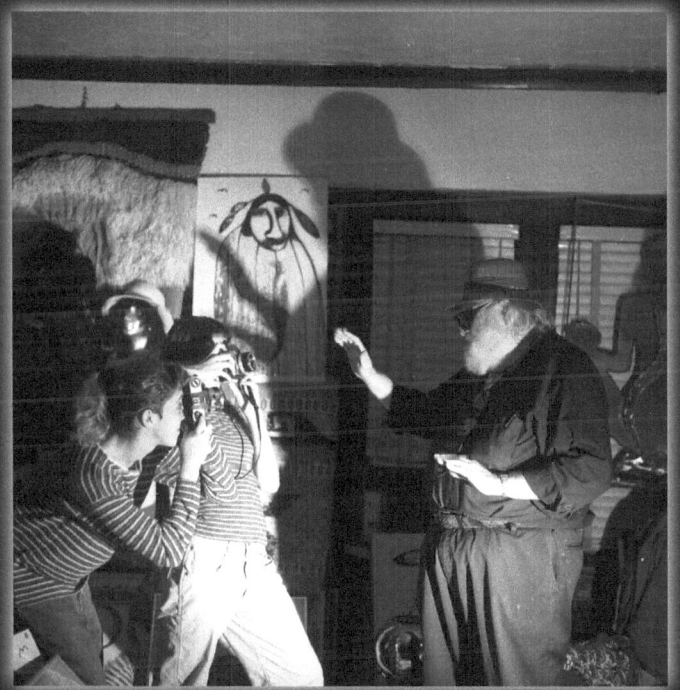

Bob Watt

IMAGE SIZE 16" H X 16" W

SILVER GELATIN PRINT

Michael Kutzer

"Punch"

● ● ● ● ● ● ● ● ● ● ● ● ● ● ● ● ●

My work varies in techniques including oil, acrylic, color pencil, gouache, etching, and woodcut. Regarding the topic, I am swinging between landscapes and still lifes, often with a symbolic undertone and more narrative works. Being narrative I prefer graphic techniques.

"Punch," in Germany called, "Kasper," played a big role in my childhood when there was no TV in Germany. My parents hadn't even a radio. I didn't miss a performance of "Kasper" coming to our city. Later I saw the Turkish "Karagoez" and the Danish "Mester Jakel," both incarnations of the same character. I began to think about the nature of this guy. As a result I created, in 1986, 12 Punch scenes in woodcut. Each piece is made with three plates: gray, red and black.

"Punch," in the original sense, is no ideal figure or positive example. He is a being with all the human passions and weaknesses, but also the power of love, sympathy and rebellion. He can be a coward terrified by his own shadow, a self-opinionated person, or a dreamer not realizing the danger behind him. Is he, marching with the soldiers, a fellow traveler, or mocking about military? In any case, he doesn't hold the mirror of truth toward us in an educational intention, but is the mirror himself.

Do you recognize yourself in some of these prints?

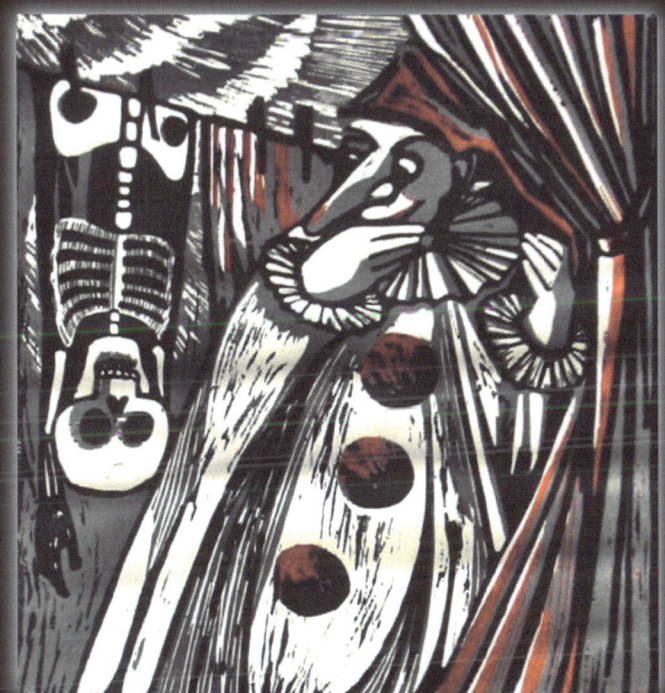

"Punch I"

Discovery

IMAGE SIZE, 11.6" H x 11.4" W

INGRES PAPER SIZE 23.7" H x 17.2" W

WOOD BLOCK PRINT

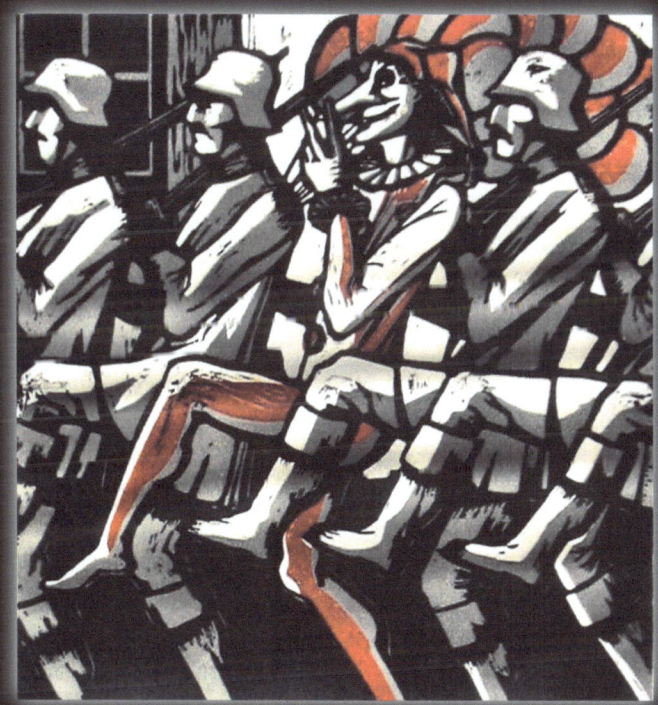

"Punch III"

In Step

IMAGE SIZE, 11.6" H x 11.4" W

INGRES PAPER SIZE 23.7" H x 17.2" W

WOOD BLOCK PRINT

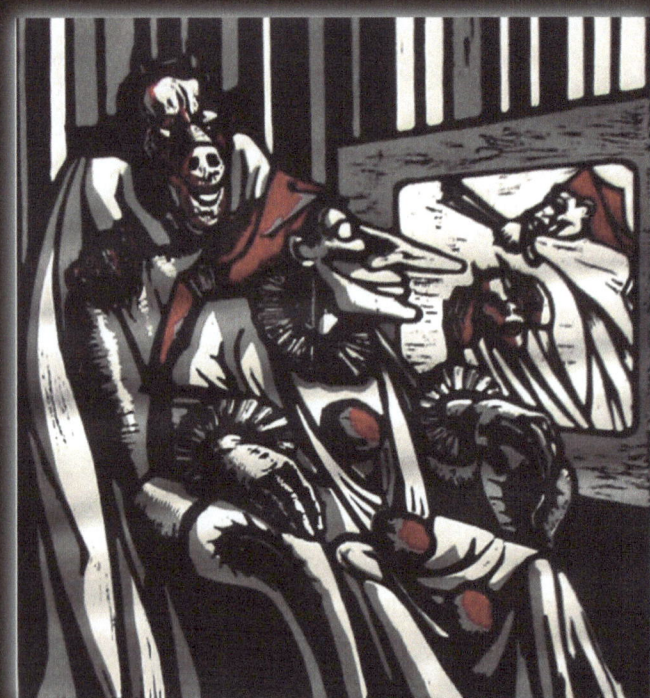

"Punch IV"

Virtual World

IMAGE SIZE, 11.6"H x 11.4"W

INGRES PAPER SIZE 23.7"H x 17.2"W

WOOD BLOCK PRINT

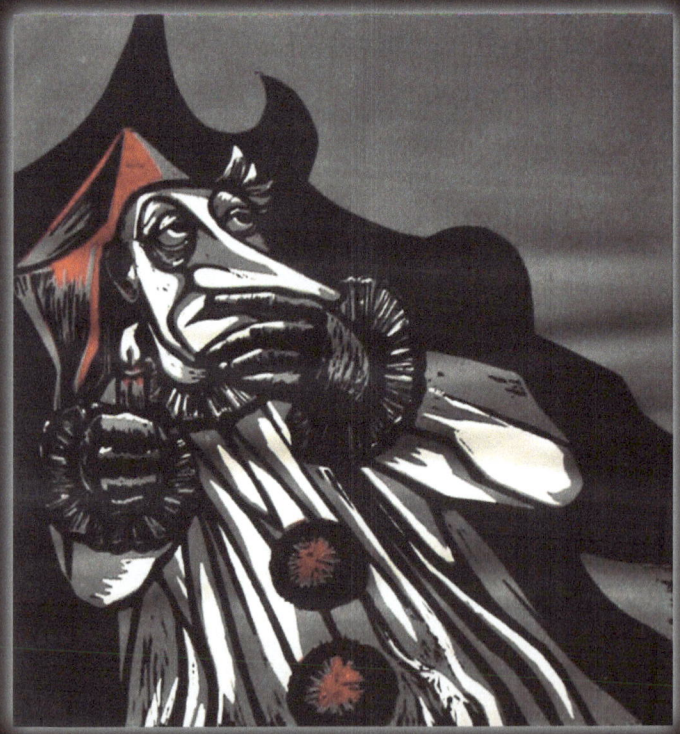

"Punch IX"

Fear

IMAGE SIZE, 11.6" H x 11.4" W

INGRES PAPER SIZE 23.7" H x 17.2" W

WOOD BLOCK PRINT

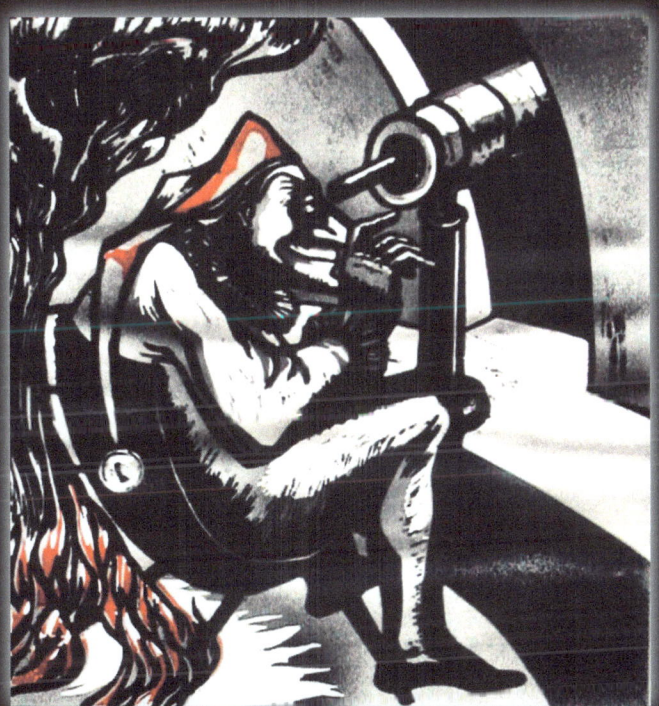

"Punch XI"

Far Sightedness

IMAGE SIZE, 11.6" H x 11.4" W

INGRES PAPER SIZE 23.7" H x 17.2" W

WOOD BLOCK PRINT

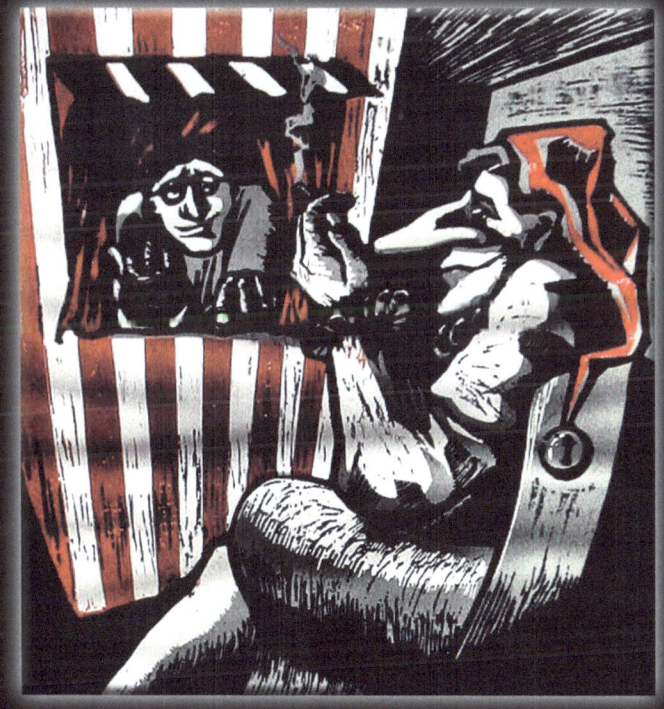

"Punch XII"

Strike

IMAGE SIZE, 11.6"H x 11.4"W

INGRES PAPER SIZE 23.7"H x 17.2"W

WOOD BLOCK PRINT

Michael Thompson

"Taxi Cabs, Amusement Rides, and Hypnosis"

My sculptures are equal part child's play, mechanical construction and whimsy. They are made with vintage Erector and Meccano building sets (the British version began manufacturing in 1901.) Exploring notions of form and function, they mingle serendipity, the rigors of design, and the limitations of the construction sets to explore the promise of the toy in the pursuit of invention.

The "Yellow" series incorporates vintage taxi top lights set upon a filigree of Erector Set bases. They proclaim their color in capital letters, yet rather than as a corporate moniker (The Yellow Cab Company), I respond to the lights as pronouncements, the simple, fundamental exclamation of a prime color.

"Tower with Green Lights" is made with the lights that surrounded the proscenium of the Chicago Theatre on State Street in the loop.

"Prow" poses a vintage bow running light and seats it proudly on a cantilevered bent- frame base, insinuating motion and thrust.

The kinetic pieces show another possibility of the materials—the ability to transform into platforms for kinetics. "Tornado" offers an abstract representation of the storm, which, with a turn of the crank begins to twist and assume the motion we associate with the storm.

"Amusement Ride" defines space within a space for the duration of the action. Transparency and form are defined by rotary movement.

"Self-Hypnosis Machine" combines rare French construction pieces with two spinning tops. Originally holding only one top, I found a second and felt compelled to redesign the piece to better cast its spell in stereo.

Yellow #2

11" H x 20" W x 7" D

ERECTOR SET PARTS AND VINTAGE TAXI SIGN

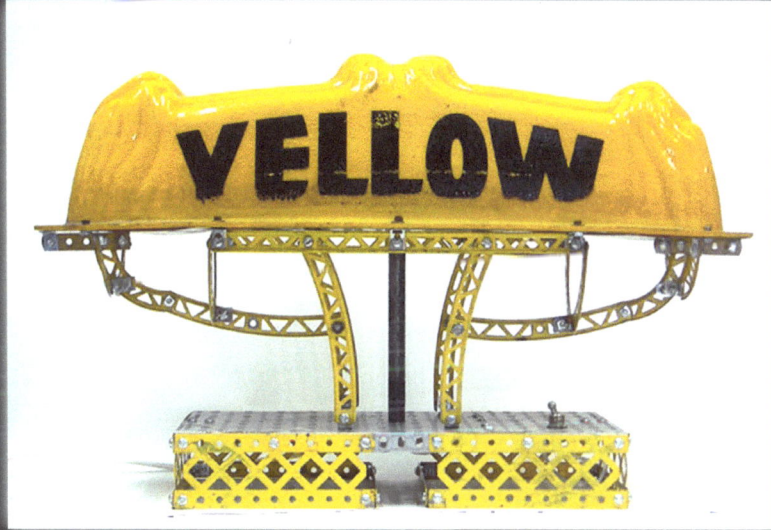

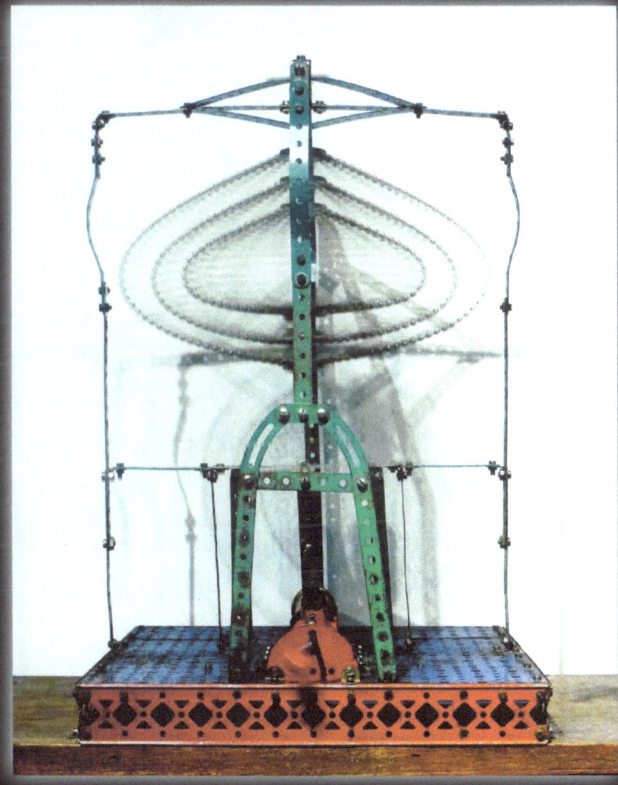

AMUSEMENT Ride

20" H x 16" W x 16" D

KINETIC SCULPTURE

ERECTOR SET PARTS AND BEADED CHAINS

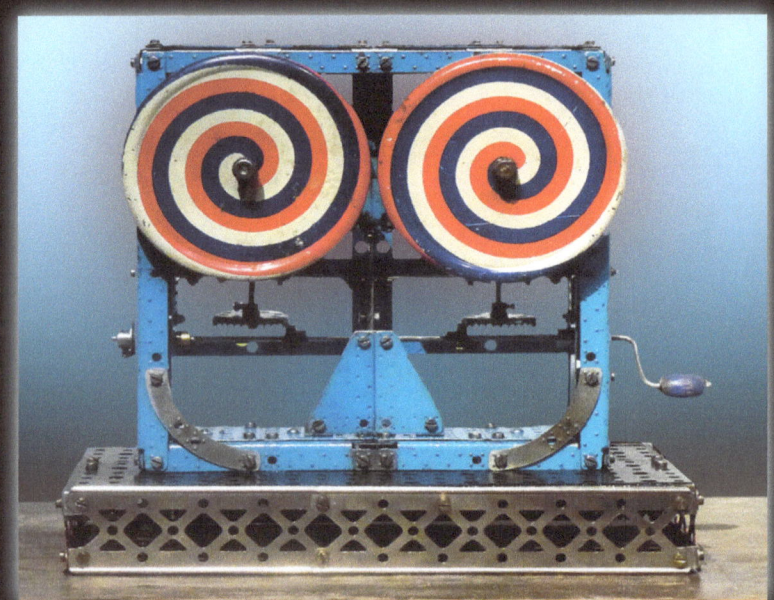

Self Hypnosis Machine

10" H x 10" W x 5" D

KINETIC SCULPTURE

ERECTOR SET PARTS AND COLORFUL WHEELS

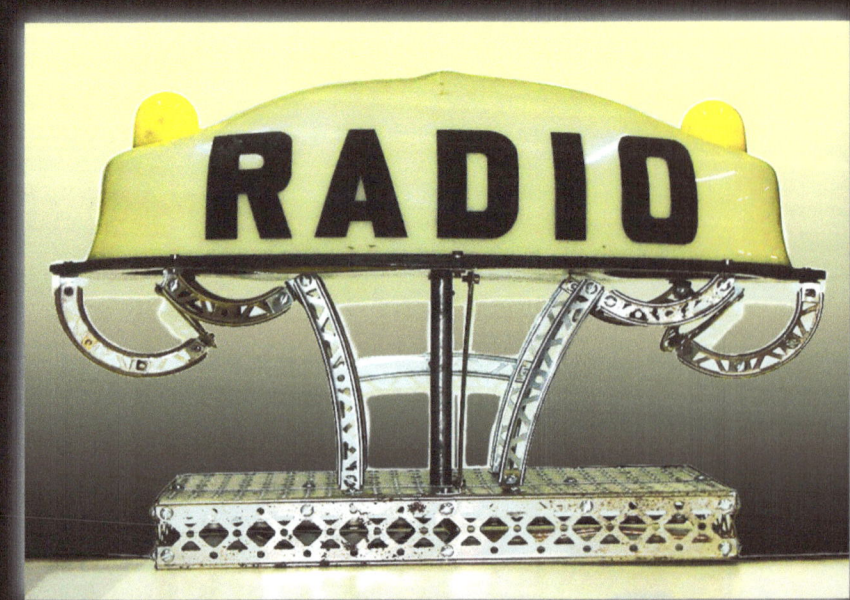

Radio Lamp

11" H x 18" W x 8" D

ERECTOR SET PARTS AND VINTAGE TAXI SIGN

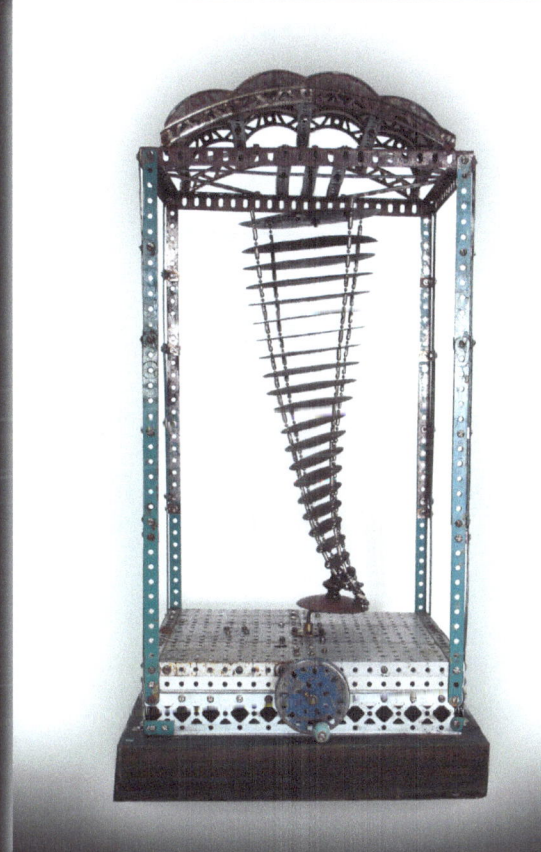

Tornado
21" H x 14" W x 14" D

KINETIC SCULPTURE WITH ERECTOR SET PARTS

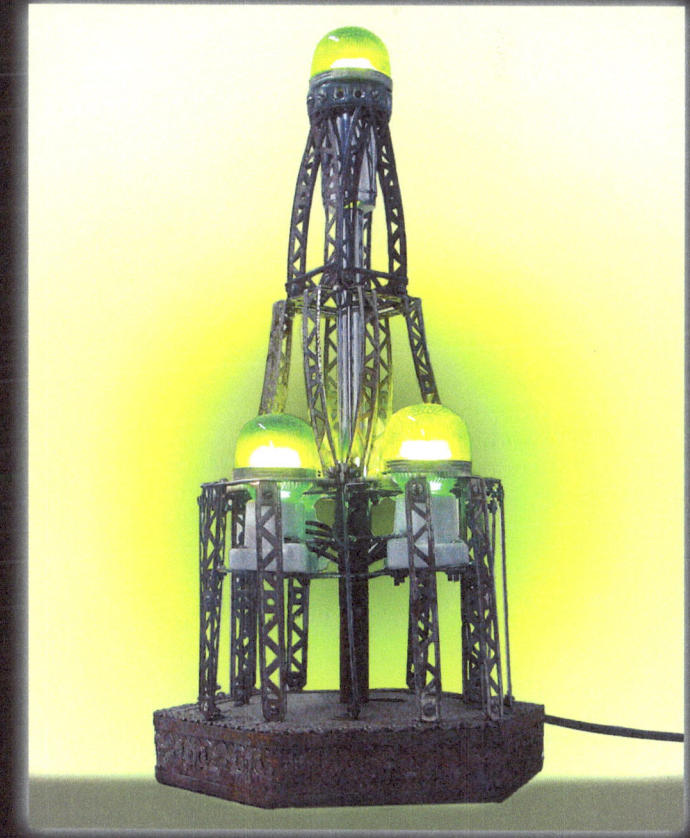

Tower with Green Lights
24" H x 10" W x 10" D

ERECTOR SET PARTS AND VINTAGE GREEN LIGHTS

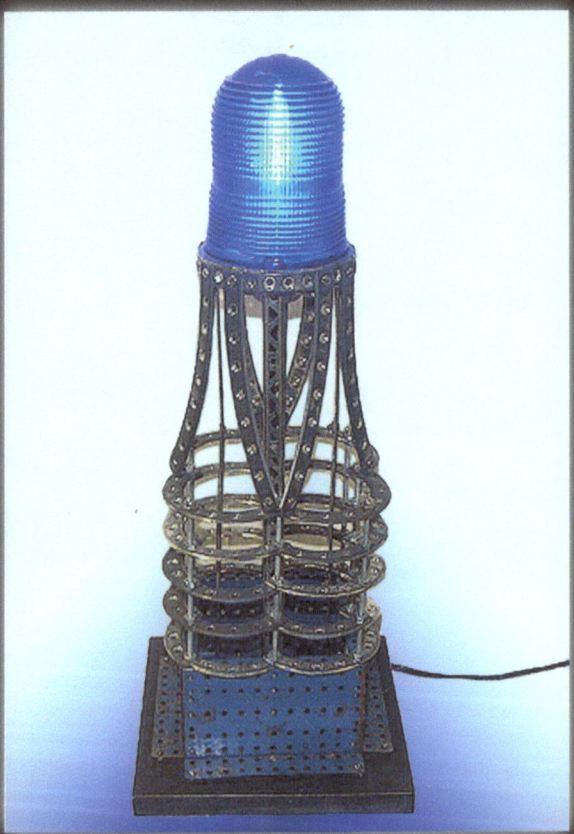

TOWER WITH BLUE LIGHT
20" H X 8" W X 8" D

ERECTOR SET PARTS AND VINTAGE BLUE GLOBE LIGHT

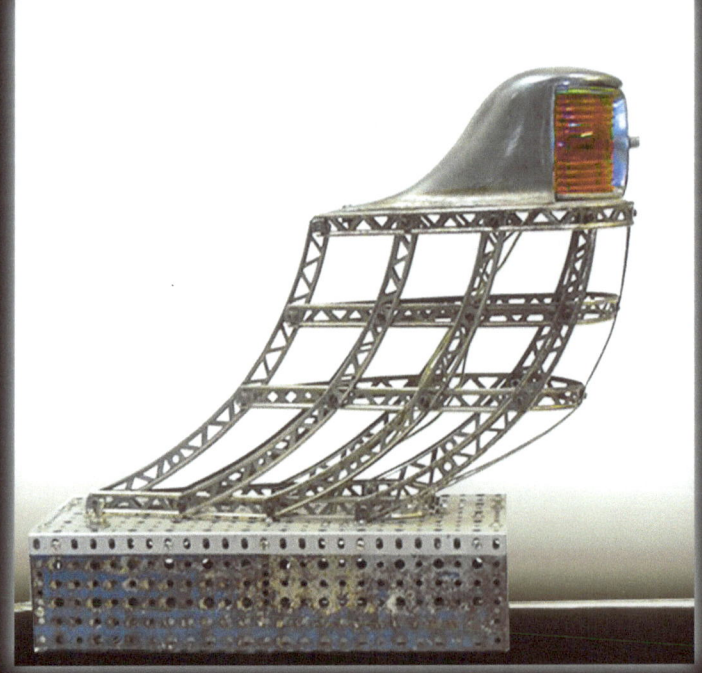

PROW
14" H X 16" W X 8" D

ERECTOR SET PARTS AND VINTAGE RED LIGHT

Timothy Cobb Fine Arts

Historic Third Ward

207 East Buffalo Street

Lobby

Milwaukee, WI 53202

Tuesday through Saturday

10 am to 5 pm

414-271-4150

timothycobbfinearts.com

tim@timothycobbfinearts.com

www.ingramcontent.com/pod-product-compliance
Lightning Source LLC
Chambersburg PA
CBHW050406180526
45159CB00005B/2167